Salvation

Interrupted

My

High!

Salvation Interrupted my High!

Copyright © Natalie Reid

ISBN: 978-1-958186-14-5

Publisher, Editor and Book Design:

Fiery Beacon Publishing House, LLC

Fiery Beacon Consulting and Publishing Group

Graphics: FBPH Graphics Team, Dashona Smith

Salvation Interrupted My High!

Natalie Reid

Table of Contents

The Dedication

The Foreword

"In the Beginning, God"

Chapter 1

Plaid, Pigtails and The Smell of Addiction   11

Chapter 2

"I Know that's Not Her on MLK!"   19

Chapter 3

The Gates are Open   26

Chapter 4

Rita   34

Chapter 5

Warning Shots   42

Chapter 6

I Can't Get Away From It   48

Chapter 7

Get Out   52

Chapter 8

No More Remnants   57

Chapter 9

A Blueprint for the Addict   62

Chapter 10

A Note to the Family   72

Chapter 11

Full Circle   81

Connect with the Author   89

The Dedication

Mom....

From the moment you found out, you were hurt, but you loved me through it. Your very presence was a constant reminder of who God had STILL created me to be. The look in your eyes wouldn't let me forget what you instilled in me and especially, the odds that I survived. Thank you for believing in me. Thank you for loving me. Thank you for reminding me. Thank you for pushing me. I love you.

To Rita....

I wish you were here to read about how God used you to impact and change my life forever.

Had it not been for you, I would have died right where I was. You were the one God used to let me know that He hadn't forgotten about me.

When others were falling victim to their addiction, you wouldn't let me go.

Thank you for being the vessel God used to save my life.

Malinda and David Brown....

Deliverance is a powerful transformation, and God used you both to do just that for me! Thank YOU for delivering me into the house of God. Your relentless efforts have produced fruit!

Apostle Michael Dixon...

Apostle, when I did not have the words to pray, you became my voice. Thank you for not counting it as robbery to pray for me and stand with me through a most difficult place! Thank YOU!

In the Beginning, God...

Hi, my name is Natalie, and I am a GRATEFUL and RECOVERED addict.

These are words that I never thought would come out of my mouth.

You see, I was born March 31, 1961, in the upper-class neighborhood to a mother who was a nurse and a father who was a master printer. I went to Catholic school all my life until the eighth grade – that is when I begged my parents to go to public school! I ended up at Lincoln Junior High School and Dudley Senior High School, where I was a cheerleader and a track star. I came up in the prestigious neighborhood of King's Forest in Greensboro, North Carolina. I had good friends and had never seen anyone or known anyone to do drugs, in or outside of my family. (I'm not saying that no one around me did it, but since I was never exposed to it, my introduction to it was stolen from me.)

Based on my upbringing, you would have never thought that addiction would be something that would come for me. From the moment of my birth, my mom and dad knew that I was a survivor, entering this world at only three pounds at birth. What made my survival even more of a miracle you ask? My parents had lost six babies before me, and one even one after me. My mother had RH negative blood and my dad had O-positive blood. Unfortunately, back in the 60's the medical field did not know how to keep the two blood types from mixing; this is what they attributed to be the issue that caused my mother to deliver stillborn children after I was born.

27 But God has selected [for His purpose] the foolish things of the world to shame the wise [revealing their ignorance], and God has selected [for His purpose] the weak things of the world to shame the things which are strong [revealing their frailty].

1 Corinthians 1:27

So, here I am, GOD'S CHOICE and now carrying the weight of mantles and callings that I NEVER asked for. There is no way that anyone could have ever convinced me that God would ever pull me from a drug-addicted life and use that decision to land me smack dab in the center of His will, but He did. From being the one people whispered about to being the one stamped by GOD, yes, that's my story.

Chapter 1

Plaid, Pigtails, and the Smell of Addiction

From my earliest childhood moments, there was nothing about me that ever said "addiction." I did not witness it in our home and was not exposed to it at an early age – in fact, I was a Catholic school student and remained as one for most of my school-aged career and until eighth grade when I begged to go to a public school. This landed me at Lincoln Junior High school and later, Dudley Senior High School where I was a cheerleader and a track star. I would not go as far to say that my parents made sure that I was not exposed to that life on purpose, but the way they raised me simply held no room for that to be my lot. My life was filled with all the things that a little girl would expect – a life filled with love and progression maybe even beyond my years from being an only child.

He's got the whole world in His hands!
He's got the whole world in His hands!
He's got the whole world in His hands!
He's got the whole world in His hands!

Even as an adult, I remember the songs of my youth. Hearing the hymns of old and watching those around me get happy off the words alone went way over my head. If you asked me now, I would tell you that it wasn't that I couldn't appreciate what they sang but I just had to live a little bit, you see! School as it is now (but less strict) was filled with all kinds of habits and customs – now we simply call it discipline. Despite any moment when I felt suffocated by what we HAD to do, deep inside I was being groomed for something great. Life in Catholic school, even with its various exposure, kept me "green" for lack of better words. I had no exposure to drugs and had never had any experience with them at all, until life happened.

You know, love can make you do crazy things. It can make you tolerate what you were never raised to and accept what your soul refuses to and for me, that was my truth. I wasn't lacking love from my parents, but that didn't mean that I never wanted love from a man. So many times, society leaves us with the impression that only the women who don't have a "daddy" at home or a father-figure around fall in traps of what love "should" be but let me tell you this – that same desire can hit a daddy's girl in a heartbeat. I had my father but please know, that a pre-requisite for addiction is NOT being absent of a father or even a father-figure in order for the addiction trap to work. As I look back, I know that every experience played its part, from being abused, misled, and diminished- instead of leaving, my goal became to help fix them in hopes that they could fix me too. The smiles, I-do's, and commitment blinded me to the point where all I wanted was what I was promised and trust, I was obviously willing to do whatever I had to in order to accomplish that goal, that dream, that childhood fantasy. Allow me to say, Daddy's girls can get in trouble, too.

Unlike others in my circle, I did not wait to get married, and did not take a lot of time to enjoy life, as they would call it. At the tender age of eighteen and in the tenth grade, I said yes. I did not say YES for love though, I agreed because I was pregnant. After all, he was my first love and there was NO reason for me to say, NO, right? So instead, I didn't say YES to myself but said YES to a man and became his wife and later, a mother too. There is a saying that goes,

"Don't invest more in the wedding than you do in the marriage."

He was young too, in his twenties to be exact. He was a wonderful provider, but a terrible husband. After all the I do's and smiles, this became my plight as the one who I professed my love to, decided to use me as his human punching bag. When he was not physically abusive, he made sure that his words pierced me like a wrecking ball, ensuring the same demise. Needless to say, being his victim did not sit well with me at all, but like many in this situation, I felt trapped and weirdly obligated to stay. While one would ask the infamous question, "why didn't you just leave," believe me, that same thought crossed my mind. Every time I wanted to leave, that cold breeze of doubt blew in. If it wasn't the doubt that captivated me, the words he spoke with every swing that took over. Despite the hits, my reality was that I loved him and maybe if I stayed, after a while, everything would work itself out.

This pursuit transformed into my decision to forsake everything else and live for him. For me, if this meant that I would have to let go of friends, I did it. If it meant that I had to disappear from him for a while, I could have retreated and found a safe haven with family, but just as quickly, embarrassment came to assure me that to do that would be the ultimate crush of pride, so I stayed. It is here that I must add this disclaimer – this generation is not like generations past. Back then, no matter WHAT was happening, the mental programming was to stay no matter what and for me, this belief system also became my truth.

Not only did I stay with him, but I also produced with him, a miracle, our baby. Anything my blessing could have witnessed is not what drove me away immediately and exiting after expansion of our family took time. Scenarios filled my mind, and all the "what if's" tried to cloud my judgement, but once I had the courage to leave, it was all gas and no brakes. I remember the fear of being caught, but also the freedom of being free and if that meant that I had to take that chance for a fresh start, I was willing to accept the risk. After ten years staying, I found the strength and courage to leave, and I did.

For years after regaining my freedom, I vowed to stay away from men, period. I stayed single and celibate – that was my resolve. Now before you give me kudos, allow me to explain: my celibacy was fueled by depression and protection. For me, the only way to never endure that life again was to stay away from it, for good, but obviously God had a different plan in mind as you will find out later. Seven years later love found me again, and much like new love, I was on cloud nine. There I was, attending North Carolina State University as a Veterinary student and doing very well for myself and there "he" was - nice, normal, kind and employed. In addition to my journey through depression, my child remained my key focus when it came to dating.

I was very protective and could not imagine what I would have done if something had happened to them because of a decision I made to date the wrong man, so I immediately eliminated the possibility until that moment. He worked there with my auntie, so I never questioned him to be considered, "good people," and if auntie could vouch for him, he had to be okay for me and mine, too. After meeting him, I figured that it was worth a try; in my mind, after all I had been through, I deserved love, but I never imagined that this love would come with a third party named crack cocaine.

Time went on and eventually, we moved in together – this is how I discovered his addiction. My new love didn't even try to hide it, but instead offered it to me like a glass of ice, cold water on a hot summer's day. While other people our age were buying homes and building a life, there I stood being offered something that had the potential to rock my whole, entire soul. I will never forget that day, when he asked me if I wanted some of the "rock" he had. I was so naïve about it, that I assumed that he was referring to the rocks in the driveway because that was all I had ever seen. Of course, during high school we smoked a little marijuana, but this invitation was completely different from the others, and I knew it. I had never seen "hard drugs" until this day; needless to say, I was officially, "green."

He asked if I wanted some, all while grabbing a soda can and repurposing it as the tool that he would eventually use to initiate a rendezvous with his "other" love. So, there he was, bringing in cans, punching holes in them and dropping what he called his "rock" on top of it. I would watch him light it up and begin smoking it through a tube in complete disbelief. This for me marked the beginning of hell. Like the abuse in my former relationship, I now transferred that loyalty to this place, no matter what I heard in the depths of my heart.

My refusal became faint, because let's be honest, what other way could I have proven my love and commitment to him and receive the love I desperately wanted in return? I watched him, moment after moment – how he prepared, how he consumed and how for that moment in time everything that could hurt him or take over him became silent in his world. Though my life had been much worse than it was in that moment, I could only imagine how the world on pause felt.

I sat there wondering, how it felt to have seemingly, no problems, worries or concern, just you and your "escape." There finally came a day when I finally gave into it, and I surrendered to it. No one ever realizes that they have crossed over into addiction until they set that "thing" off. It does not come looking for you, but instead, looks for you to initiate it, and once you do, its goal becomes taking you on the ride of a lifetime. Slowly but surely, I realized that with addiction, one encounter would be too many, but one million encounters would never be enough.

It bears repeating.....

Even Daddy's Girl gets in trouble.

Chapter 2

"I Know That's Not Her on MLK!"

Smoke filled the room while the escape became my temporary reality. I never imagined that this would be me, and yet every time guilt hit, my addiction became my answer. As with anything we begin, my habit eventually went from the inside of me to the outside of me. When I first began, hiding it took work, but it was worth the reward of the high I would receive as payment. Eventually, I no longer cared who knew or even who saw; the corner of Martin Luther King Jr. Boulevard and McConnell Road became my new "spot."

My addiction became my pursuit, yes you heard it right, my pursuit. Even when I should have been chasing other things, at the mention of my addiction everything else took a back seat. I graduated if you will, from sharing a hit with my love to now, having my own supplier. It did not matter what I had to give up, I just wanted the high. Let me share this – like anything else, after you take in something for a while, eventually, that's no longer enough and you begin to require more to get the high you had during your first encounter. An addict is always chasing the feeling of the FIRST high, and after being irritated about the outcome, eventually settles for whatever high they can get.

Eventually, the news spread far and wide, that Natalie had become an addict. This habit did not hit me in a town that never knew me but, in a place where many had known me just about all my life. I hid it for as long as I could, but there came a day where I became careless without caution. Of course, in the back of my mind, how my family and friends would react periodically entered my mind, but in that same space, the justification of my addiction spoke up to remind me of why "we" were in a relationship. There indeed comes a moment when an addict chases their addiction so far, that in their mind, they have arrived at the point of no return.

They have stolen all they can steal. They have lied all they can lie. They have covered all they can cover.

They have embraced what they defend with an unrighteous heart.

Everyone else's opinion no longer held weight, but there was something about the reaction of my mother that stung. Here was this woman, one who made sure that I was raised right and gave me her everything on the behalf of my other siblings who didn't make it, now faced with the harsh reveal that her daughter had become a drug addict. Among all her responses, the one that sits with me the most was her confusion with how I ended up in that space. No matter the age, Mama is still Mama and especially on this day, that mantle did not fall. There she was, confused about how it happened to me.

"What did I do?"

"What did I miss?"

"What could I have done?"

She embraced the responsibility of my movements as if she carried me while addicted therefore leaving me no choice outside of becoming an addict myself. Confusion became her garment as she pondered how it could have EVER been me. This disbelief was not limited to a conversation, but the community's response. Word of my "hanging out" on MLK circulated like breaking news. Stories got back to my home front that I had become addicted to the point of literally flagging down cars in a wild attempt to get my high filled. I was willing to tell whatever lie I needed to get a hold of that high that captivated me. Nothing was going to stop me from that.

Not loss.

Not embarrassment.

Nothing.

I was going to get to my high, no matter what it took to get it.

This became my personal goal, until the day that my supplier died. I had planned for everything else – how I would get my high and how I would get higher the next time, but I never planned for what I would do if my supplier died. In my mind, it just didn't seem like a possibility but here I was on the verge of another high, with no supply, leaving the street as my only resolve. What amazed me beyond people's reaction, was how they had no solutions but all of the criticisms. The community knew I was on the street and recognized exactly who I was, but no one pulled over on the side of the road in an attempt to save me from this monster who had overtaken every part of my life.

When my father and my mother forsake me, Then the LORD will take care of me.

Psalm 27:10

My parents didn't forsake me, but at that moment, I felt as if the community did. I was a sheep thrown in a wolf's cage, chasing after the addiction but inwardly praying that someone would look beyond my chase and see ME. Yes, I was willing to do whatever I had to, and yet the greater one inside of me never abandoned me. I was willing to trust anyone that I had to just to get that high in my system. I had been raped for it, stolen from for it, but none of that mattered to me. Despite my addiction, GOD never abandoned me but constantly reminded me that He had me in his hands, addiction, habits, and all.

Anyone that knew my path back then would probably ask,

"How did God have you? The church you passed by on a daily wouldn't even touch you!"

While this was true, there was something about knowing that someone even greater than the people that claimed Him but ignored me, had my name on His heart. Walking that path became a constant reminder that I was doing wrong, and that God expected better out of me. The sights, the sounds, and the cross, were all magnified before me. One day, I remember walking my normal path. On this day there was nothing about seeing the church that day that brought a smile to my face, but instead in that moment, hostility.

"God, why won't you stop me?"

I yelled it to the top of my lungs. I didn't care who saw me or what their response would be. After all, everyone had their opinion and would just be able to add this to their list of "tea." I waited because Lord knows I was demanding a response. Right when I was on the verge of giving up, I heard just as strong as I delivered it,

"Because you have chosen this!"

Needless to say, this was not the answer I was expecting and, in my view, not the answer that I wanted either. I wanted to hear God tell me that He knew it wasn't my fault and He was coming in to take it all away. I wanted Him to tell me that I wouldn't have to work my way out of this, but instead, just float out the same way I floated in. I wanted Him to take it as His own like my mother did when she found out, but He wouldn't.

God wasn't abandoning me.

He wasn't forgetting me.

He just demanded that I take responsibility.

Maybe it was the guilt of walking by the church that overtook me or the silence of the members who looked at me with disgust. Maybe it was the pride of refusing to accept the part that I played in this detour of my life.

Regardless of what drew me, God was about to use it for His glory.

Chapter 3

The Gates are Open

18 "And I also say to you that you are Peter, and on this rock I will build My church, and the gates of Hades shall not [g]prevail against it."

Matthew 16:18

Natalie, "birth of the Lord." You would think that with a name like that, life would not have the ability to hit so hard, but for me it felt as if this reality only became a target in my back. Regardless of my movements, I knew that God still loved me; He proved that every time I survived a high. Even as I reflect in this moment, I can't even imagine how many situations God really saved me from. I can't even count how many times the angels assigned to my life had to fight for me, but I hope and pray that this chapter will give you insight into just a few instances to which I am privy.

There is nothing strange about an addicted person losing themselves amid a high. Just as there are functioning alcoholics, this has the same potential as the high is embraced while life still makes its demands clear. Even during the high, sometimes you just want to lay down and enjoy the "escape." One day, that was me – I just wanted to lay down, so I stopped to visit one of my friends at their house. I was beyond high at this point, life had drained me, and for once I just wanted some level of peace. So, there I was taking in a moment that I desired with all my heart, just to feel safe and free to rest until I heard a voice.

"You think she's sleep?"

This couldn't be real. Even in what should be the safest of places, I found myself now completely unsafe all over again. There was no time to wait or to talk sense into anybody, there was only time to fight and that is exactly what I did. My friend didn't come to my aid, it was me and "them," and I refused to be added to their list of accomplishments. I swung, I fought, until I got out. For me this was enough, but little did I know that my fight was just beginning. That is the thing with the life of an addict, they have to come into it willing to fight. There is no pretty exchange in this life and, matter of fact, life itself can oftentimes feel like a horror movie, as it did with this next memory, I want to share with you.

I just wanted to get where I had to go, nothing more and nothing less. Regardless of my desires, that did not stop the murderer that came for me that day. I was minding my own business, only to be invaded by a man with a knife demanding that I drive. I knew he didn't just want my car or a ride down the road, but he wanted my life, and I refused to allow him to leave with it. He yelled and screamed while laying down his demands. I knew that if I didn't get out soon, I would be added to the list of his plans so I did the only thing I could think of, I jumped out of the car. All I was thinking was getting out, that's all I wanted; what I didn't consider was the seat belt still connected and holding me in the car. Now it would be one thing if the car was in park, but even in my attempt to save my life, the car was not in park but instead in drive. The car proceeded forward as it dragged me up the road.

"God please don't let me die, not like this!"

I can't even pinpoint the prayers that exited my soul, and even my offender for a moment probably feared for me too, I don't know. We weren't in an isolated place, so I screamed for help, but help never showed up for me. I have no idea how it happened, but during the altercation, the wheel turned and the same car that held my life in its hands ended up in a ditch. As it inched towards its resting place, it slowed down just enough for me to free myself from the seatbelt and the car. Once again, the community watched my demise as I eventually made eye contact with an old classmate of mine.

"Didn't you hear me yelling for help?"

He didn't budge. He didn't even come over to see if I was okay. He only kept walking as I remained there in shock and mutilated on the day that could have been marked as my death. His ill-response left me stilled in time, but only for a moment. I quickly snapped back into my moment only to realize the murderer had too, even to the point of jumping out of the car and coming for me again. All I knew to do was run,

There was no help in sight.

There was no safe place.

All I could do was run.

I ran down the street, banging on doors, just trying to get someone to help me. One house answered but wouldn't open their door to help me but instead said that they would call the cops for me. I ran for my LIFE and while others would just reflect on why I ran, I soon realized that the level of what I was going through was directly related to the greatness that God had embedded on the inside of me. I wish I could say that I didn't have any other encounters and that everything after that was smooth sailing, but sadly that is not the case. I use "sadly" loosely, for as I share more here, I realize EVEN the more, that I made it. Among the things that were taken from me, and the feeling of safety that had become non-existent for me, losing my sight became one of the most pivotal experiences I encountered.

Life made me a fighter; I had been one since I came out of my mother's womb. This day, the fighter in me had to show up once more as an altercation brewed between a man and I. Fighting for me had become like second nature and believe me when I say, I refused to go out without my victory in hand. One thing that was always revealed to me was that many of those who came for me came with hopes of taking my very life. On this day, I found myself fighting for my life again. Based on who I had become, it didn't make sense for anyone to come seeking MY life.

I hadn't done anything to anyone in my view.

I just wanted to get high, in peace.

Fists swung and breathing intensified. I was determined to leave with my life and refused to believe that all of the fighting I had endured would end in defeat this day. As he swung, he connected, but not to my face but instead to my eye. His hit scratched the surface of my eye.

Somehow, I got away, and immediately went to the hospital. I knew that something was wrong, but the hospital told me that everything was just fine. I knew in my heart that it wasn't, but I took their word and left. For about four days, I walked around knowing that something was wrong but refusing to go back, until I couldn't take it anymore and was convinced to go back and try again. This is where I received the news that due to the amount of damage done to my eye, I would have to lose it in order to have a chance at a normal life. Addiction doesn't care how you get "it" as long as you get it. This life is willing to take chances that SHOULD end in your absolute demise and leave you knowing that if it doesn't, it was only by the grace of God that it didn't – this next story falls into this very category. It is one thing to give yourself away willingly but takes a different turn when it's taken from you.

Remember, I didn't care how I got my high filled, as long as it was mine. If that meant I had to steal, then I did it. If I had to lay down, then I would – I just wanted my high. It was this approach that showed me that monsters don't look like monsters at all, but like regular people like you and me. They don't have a sign that says, "I will rape you," or "I will kill you," but sometimes carry a sign or a conversation that says, "do you need a ride somewhere?" This day, my answer was yes – whatever it took to win my chase, I was down for it. To this day I cannot tell you what the man's name was – I just knew that he was talking right and could get me to what I needed in the moment. You can always tell what a driver "wants," and this day whatever he was looking for I was down for. I told him where to go, but eventually the car traveled in an entirely different direction leaving me helpless and without a voice.

"You picked the wrong car today."

This unknown man drove me around the city of Greensboro for what had to be hours at gunpoint. Even if I wanted to scream I couldn't, because I never knew the moment that I would go too far, and he would pull the trigger. There was no calling anyone or yelling for help as we were too far away for anyone to hear me and even if we had been within reach, who would jump at the opportunity to help me, an addict? He drove to the woods. As he continued down the path, I had already resolved my mind that either I would fight or die that day. I knew that there was no one in sight and that kind of isolation could only end a couple of different ways. For whatever reason, instead of him carrying out his plan, do you know what he said?

"I think I'm gonna take you back to where I got you from."

He had every intention on killing me, but he didn't! Let me be very clear – this man had a plan, but why he didn't do it, I can only attribute to God! To this day, there is nothing that anyone can tell me to make me believe that he shifted because he felt bad or out of respect for me; none of these possibilities were true. There were at least four attempts on my life that I can quickly recall, four, but none of them prospered, NONE.

Only by God's power am I still here!

He's got the whole world in His hands. He's got the whole world in His hands. He's got the whole world in His hands.
He's got the whole world in His hands!

Chapter 4

Rita

Recovery is defined as "a return to a normal state of health, mind or strength." In all honesty, I saw no return in sight. I had hit the lowest of the lows and could not figure out how to get out of the hole I had created for myself. I was desperate, I was determined, but I was still called and chosen, too.

The day I went to use after my supplier died, I walked outside looking to make my next connect only to be greeted by a woman lying in front of my apartment. Prior to her assumed position, she had even gotten to the point of walking around in the parking lot shouting, "The world has come to an end!" I had seen so much by this point, that I just assumed that she was just another addict like me, so I proceeded to get past her and keep moving. People knew about me, but truth be told, I was glad to have someone else become the conversation of the complex. As soon as it seemed like I had accomplished my mission and had gotten past her, she jumped up.

"Are you saved?"

Wait. What? Am I...saved? Here was this lady, someone I had never interacted with, and she wanted to know if I was saved? No matter how hard I tried to get away, she had me in her salvation clutches and would not let go. Hours passed by while she went on and on in conversation with me (I really should say conversation by herself, because I had long since checked out.) As the days passed, I came to understand that the disgruntled look on my face or even the attempt to look as irritated as possible when she would show up, was not enough to make her stop. Once I gave her a second of my time, for her it became an open door and an open opportunity. Every day there she was with hours of conversation in tow. If I tried to hide, meaning, if I tried to turn off lights, tv, etc. or stop every movement I was making altogether, she would always speak through the door and say,

"I see you."

I see you. While I could say that was her speaking to me, I have to wonder if that was God just letting me know, too. The addiction to the addiction can make you want to run and hide, only to one day be faced with your own fears and

35

tears. I had far surpassed feeling the threats of being "seen," but there was something about THIS instance of being seen that continued to replay in my mind. Every day that I came out of the house, she was there. I was just trying to get to my supply, but this woman wasn't having it! It didn't matter what excuse I made up, she refused to allow me to simply pass. It didn't matter how many duck and dodge routines I formulated, this lady would be right there for it, ready to let me know that God saw me and so did she.

One day, I decided that she would be my "donor" for the day. Believe it or not there I was preparing my spill for a deal and this lady, who I came to know as Rita, was going to be the one I would use today. I didn't have to dodge her that way, but instead only had to release the unmistakable request for money. I didn't offer a reason for why I needed it, and she didn't ask. Matter of fact the moment I asked her she said,

"I'm not even going to ask what you need the money for, but if I give it to you, you've got to go to church with me."

As I considered everything else I did just to get a high, this to me was no different. She wanted me to go to a place that, in my eyes, never tried to rescue me from my addiction. Despite my many disgruntlements, one thing I knew was not to lie to God. As she waited for my reply, my response went from refusal to reply. Rita got her way; I was going to church with her and there was no backing out of it. The sounds of church – the people, the praises and the songs filled the atmosphere where we sat. I must admit that I didn't expect to walk in and just be a "part" of the service. Even if no one was looking at me, it felt like the whole room full of people were. My paranoia, though loud, could not trump my sleep. Yeah, you guessed it, I slept through the whole service like a baby who had just consumed cereal added to her milk. Despite the sound and even the sermon, nothing could interrupt this divine rest that I had encountered. Before I knew it, the altar call had come and just like that I was awake.

"Does anyone want to get saved?"

After a whole service full of sleep, I knew that they could not be referring to me. The music played and the preacher continued with his appeal. There I sat, fresh out of sleep wondering how long this person was going to wait before coming up; they were taking their sweet time, and I had a whole high to get to. My mind knew to stay seated, but I guess my legs didn't get the memo; before I knew it, there I was, both feet planted and now to the church, identified as the one they were waiting for. Everything in me wanted to let them know that they had it wrong, that I was just tired and ready to go, but before I had the chance to even plead my case,

"Do you believe Romans 8?"

"Yes."

The questions continued. At this point my flesh resounded from within, "Forget everything about not lying to get out of a discipleship moment and get me out of here!" Flesh heard me loud and clear, but the preacher was still going through the confession of faith and waiting for my responses.

Yes.

Yes.

Yes, now can I go home please?!

I didn't even take time to turn and look at Rita's face, but I'm sure that her expression was priceless and undoubtedly celebratory. I already knew that she had NO plans of allowing me to live this down! She HAD to see me asleep, right? She HAD to know that I didn't mean to get up like that – I mean I wasn't coming to the altar, I was just ready to go. She knew that, right? Even if she did, I knew she didn't care; in her eyes an ember had been lit and she was determined to turn it into a Holy Ghost forest fire and what better way to start that, then by way of the next question the preacher asked:

"So, who invited you to church today?"

Reluctantly, I told him, that it was Rita, the "Fire Starter." When I shared this news, do you know what happened next? He charged HER with the task of discipling ME. This woman - the one who laid out on my walkway and made sure that everyone in the neighborhood knew that the end was coming, was now responsible for the maturity of my soul!

Whatever it took, I no longer cared.

Just let me go home to my high.

Rita took the charge seriously. It wasn't for credit – this push was for my soul. No matter how much I fell off after that day, she never allowed me to forget the decision that I made, willingly or not. It wasn't her swinging a bible in my face that reminded me, sometimes it was just her presence or her just showing there at the times when I needed her even though I didn't want to admit it. I often wondered why she didn't just let me go.

I knew that I wasn't the only addict that received Christ and went right back to their addiction moments after the decision; news of women being found murdered and receiving word of friends dying from my very bondage was proof of that. They like me, were doing what they had to do just to relive that first moment that by then had become bigger than life to me. She invested time into me like she owed me! She stayed with me just like the preacher instructed her to do and every time I tried to give her a reason why she SHOULD have left or that she shouldn't have dealt with me, do you know what she did?

She encouraged me.

She began speaking to the greater inside of me no matter what she saw or even smelled. She never gave up on me.

"You will preach this Word," she would say with full conviction.

Rita, I will forever thank God for you.

Thank you.

Chapter 5

Warning Shots

If visions had a sound upon impact, it would sound like an epic explosion between life and choices. Have you ever had the feeling that your body and your soul were being completely separated? If not, let me tell you, I have, and it is a bona fide experience.

There I was, incoherent but present for what I will simply call The Ascension. This vision did not even bother to take me to Heaven, but instead, Hell. The screams were undeniable and the smell irrefutable. My exhaustion gave me a first-class tour of Hell. Levels upon levels were revealed to me, as people received varying degrees of punishment based on their sins. No matter how bad the sins were, the screams were deafening and merged like the ingredients of a melting pot. The punishment became more and more severe, as they sat on one level of torture and dropped to another right before the glass doors closed on them to ensure their capture. Every time I thought that there were no more levels to go, they dropped again. Their cries for help turned into screeches and squeals, and there

I was, unable to do anything to help them. They screamed for help, they wanted me to rescue them, but there I remained helpless to them or even myself. The tour did not stop there, though I wish it had. Though I have never seen Satan, in this vision he became clear as day. Standing behind a wall, I saw glimpses of eyes and scales peeking through the partition that divided us. He was there, but I knew that he could come no further as he looked, paced, and waited.

Now you would probably think that waking up from a vision like this would be just the wake up call I needed, but I must be honest and tell you that you're wrong. For me there was only one response to what I had encountered and that was, to go after another hit. What puzzled me the most you ask?

God allowed me to see it, but never stopped me from using.

I could rehearse the dream I had one million times or more, but even that could not stop me from seeking what I had deemed irreplaceable. You see, that's how ignorant we can be. God will show us something, give us every red flag imaginable and still we decide to reside with our selfish motives and behaviors. Now don't get me wrong, this was not the first "sign" that I was going the wrong way. God sent several signs from day one but none of them were enough to make me stop feeding the monster I had given permission to live within. God allowed me to peek into hell, just to confirm my suspicions that it was real, and if I didn't change my ways, it would eventually be for me.

I have to admit, I was glad that no one really knew me in church the day that I said "yes" to God; had they known they would have expected the change I criticized myself for not immediately manifesting. I got home that day and looked in the mirror.

"I don't look any different."

While we are here, allow me this moment to share with you the reality of addiction – THIS RECOVERY takes WORK! I stood in the mirror waiting to look like what I had subjected my body to never happened, only to realize that recovery would not happen without the work! There I stood, looking at me, expecting the "addict" to simply disappear, but she was still there, so why not feed her? Without hesitation and my "yes" coming along for the ride, I grabbed my drugs and my tools and took a trip to what we call, "The Grove." For me, this was a safe haven where I could get high in peace – no Rita, no parents, no peeping neighbors in my business, just me and my vice. I knew that this was just the moment I needed, and let's be honest, petitioned for even from the altar of the church.

First hit.

"See the blood of her soul is on your hands."

I looked around at all the other women in the house getting high with me, but none of them were talking to me – they were so high they barely even knew that I was in the room. It had to be the hit I took. There was no way that God had shown up in the very place that I felt He would never come. I looked around, but no one else responded; no one else heard what I had just heard outside of me.

"Just don't let me die! Lord, let me make it out!"

Others in my space looked over at me as if I were going crazy! Flashes of my friends who died from the same "hit" flashed across my mind; it was then knew that maybe, just maybe, God had had enough. Was my hit laced? Did someone do something to it? No, it was Him, and my soul knew it.

"You had the opportunity to come to Me and here you sit doing the same thing they are doing when you should be ministering to them?"

I knew I had to leave the house before things got massively worse. The others just kept looking at me; all I could see was what I was supposed to say to them but how could I minister to them and smoke with them, too. It wasn't possible. High and all, I finally made it out of the house and down the steps only to be greeted by a huge shadow nearby.

I looked around.

Nothing.

There was nothing that had the capacity or ability to produce what I saw in that moment. Yea, it could have only been Him, it could have only been God. I came out of the house that day knowing that the high I had prepared my mind for all day had amounted to nothing at that moment.

"That JESUS! That man done messed up my high!"

Who I had been just minutes before and the excuses adopted, no longer meant anything. I turned and went right back in that house; euphoria restored and began releasing these words:

"Jesus is coming back."

It did not matter that I had just smoked right over there in that spot and honestly, it did not matter if I smoked again when I left, the fire of the Holy Ghost took over everything about me and spoke a Word that I felt completely unqualified to release. In that window of time, what I had done no longer mattered, and the same God that I heard about came to a place I never expected Him to show up in. While others talked and were afraid to approach me, there was God speaking to me and through me. The house I stood in became an altar as I released the seed of the Word which would later become my life's purpose.

Jesus....is coming back.

Chapter 6

I Can't Get Away from It!

Decisions, decisions. It seemed as if God had shared with His servants that I had said YES but forgot to tell them WHY I said yes! In that moment I didn't want Him, I just wanted my goal. He took a moment of solace and turned me into a whole vessel preaching His Word before a room full of smoke and addiction. I was shocked that He used me, just not shocked, or even honored enough to stop what had become my passion. Addiction heard my sermon too I guess, but even that wasn't enough for it to let me go.

Regardless of how I felt, God honored my half-asleep yes and treated it as a full one. I will never forget the day I met this man who God had shared my "secret acceptance" with. I don't remember seeing him at the church, but he wasted no time making my decision known to me. Day after day and moment after moment, he made sure that he reminded me of my decision to follow God every chance he got. One day, I saw him driving up and down my street and by then I had decided within myself that he had taken it too far.

It's one thing to call me out.

It's one thing to keep my decision in front of me and sabotage my high.

It's another thing when you begin interrupting the place, I call home.

So, there he was, coming through like a drive by looking for a target. After a short time of watching him, I finally decided that enough was enough. I charged into the street and jumped in front of his car! Now, you may call me crazy, but in that moment, I was completely irritated. I was beyond done with his calling me out on the carpet and refusing to just let me be (some of you in this day and time would call it pride.)

"What…. are…. YOU….doing?!?"

He was pouring anointing oil along the path as he drove, that's what. As he later stated, he was doing it to help ME find my way back to God.

"Before I formed you in the womb I knew you;
Before you were born I sanctified[a] you;

I [b]ordained you a prophet to the nations."

Jeremiah 1:5

There I was, not caught between a rock and a hard place, but between my habit and my call. He was the constant echo in my ear that reminded me of who God had charged me to be whether I wanted to or not. He was the one God used in those precious moments to let me know that no matter how far I strayed, God would send someone to always remind me of who I was. It was the Words and the oil that trailed along my neighborhood that reminded me that I was predestined.

I wasn't just the sole survivor of my parents, I was called, chosen, and set apart to be used for God's glory.

I had more disqualifiers than a little bit, but God never neglected to let me know what He was demanding of me. As it was with me, so it is with you. Whether you are a recovering addict or you know someone who is, know that God is sending the echo right now. He is sending just the confirmation you need or even sending YOU to be the confirmation, as a reminder that even in your worst places, you are still called to the greatness embedded on the inside of you.

Remember………

[3] Every place that the sole of your foot will tread upon I have given you, as I said to Moses.

Joshua 1:3

Breathe. It's time to recover!

Chapter 7

GET OUT!

For me, the constant reminders of God's call on my life became a resuscitator and while I wish that I could say that the visions, dreams, and confirmations were enough to make me stop, it wasn't. For years after the encounter I had at church, I continued to use. Truthfully, I could not make sense of it.

I had witnessed friends die from the same addiction I embraced. I had seen more hearses drive by than a little bit and knew they died from addiction.

But I still didn't stop.

This is the place where grace became evident and believe me, I was going to ride it until the wheels fell off. For me, it felt like grace didn't care about my addiction, not to that extent. Regardless of how many times I used, God kept me! There were days where I just knew I wouldn't wake up the next day only to be greeted by the sun, the sound of birds or a nudge telling me it was time to go. The stench of the spaces I occupied filled the air, and let's be honest, no matter how much perfume spray you use, that smell is embedded in the walls forever. The same God that used me, high or not, was the same God who served as the constant reminder that I had an opportunity to come out and come forth!

> **43 Now when He had said these things, He cried with a loud voice, "Lazarus, come forth!"**
>
> **John 11:43**

Can you imagine how the people would have reacted if Lazarus had not responded to Jesus' voice? They had already begun mourning and planning for the official pronouncement of death, as many did with me as well. He called my name, I heard Him, but refused to respond; regardless, my neglect didn't take away any God-ability my Father possesses! Thank God for His patience – for how He could send so many signs and yet keep me through my own personal ignorance. Hallelujah to my God!

Regardless of all of the friends I lost, thank God there was one who remained who just happened to be my best friend. Along with all the other reminders of God's hand on my life, she stood as proof of His power, being one who God had saved and kept! Three days, three, I stayed in my house. I didn't come out and had no desire to, but instead just wanted to be left alone. After I decided to come out of my cave, I walked outside and there she was with her Husband, sitting, and waiting for me. She was tired of seeing me in this cycle, and so as any bestie would do, she came to my rescue to pull me out.

"God told me to come get you."

She said it with such conviction and power; on top of that, I knew that she was telling the whole entire truth. I knew that my grace was running out – that was part of what kept me in the house. I didn't know how to respond at first, because I knew that her making that appeal to me meant that the life I had adopted had to come to an end if I drove off with her. "Give me an hour and come back," I said. She looked, she paused and then hesitantly agreed. She didn't want to leave me there and I knew it. I knew that the way I reacted was not the way it was supposed to go, at least not in her head, nevertheless she obliged and left.

An hour passed and my best friend returned.

"Get in the car, Natalie."

I knew that she loved me, but I also knew what detox was like, and quite honestly, that scared me. I had already heard the stories and seen it in the movies too and between those two visuals, there was no part of me that wanted to go through that. I knew that if I got in that car with her, life would change forever, and I had to be ready to embrace it. I knew that getting in that car meant that I would have to feel the consequences of what I had put my body through, and I couldn't guarantee that it would be as forgiving as God had been with me. She continued to tell me to get into the car until her Husband interjected. **"Don't force her into the car!"**

The truth is this whole time I felt like I had been pushed. I felt pushed into taking my first hit. I felt pushed into giving God my first yes and now I was instinctively waiting for their push, too because after all, being pushed into decisions makes it easier, right? It was at this moment that I realized that I would have to choose, finally choose. Making a choice wasn't foreign to me because every time I chose to take a hit, I did just that. Every time I chose to embrace my addiction, I chose it.

I chose it.

Another hour passed, and there they sat, telling me that I needed to get in the car. The thing about our relationship was this – even when I didn't speak it, she felt me and she knew where I was, so I did what I was used to doing.

I told her that if she wanted me to be rescued for real, that she would pull off as soon as I got in the car.

That moment felt like a Wild, Wild West standoff, but I knew who would win so I finally conceded and got in the car. Without a moment of hesitation, we pulled off. This rescue if you will felt like a woman being rescued from her abusive mate – it was time perfectly, and when given permission executed swiftly. As we pulled off, what I had known to be life was over.

What I had known to be my addiction could be no more.

Chapter 8

No More Remnants

The ride to Pinehurst, North Carolina, felt long, but necessary. I had just made one of the hardest decisions of my life, and honestly had no idea how I would survive beyond it. So many times, we can agree on a thing, but desire to carry the remnants of that thing with us. I was in the car, wrapping my mind around the decision I had just made when a demand was presented to me – to get rid of my pipes and anything I had on me that gave me access to what I had just turned away from by getting in the car.

As beautiful as this "act" sounded, it did not come without warfare and a fight. Let me stop here and say, that though addiction comes with its physical dispositions, it is not absent of spiritual battles both seen and unseen. It was then that I realized that the enemy didn't care where I was – he wanted me addicted and eventually, dead. Without a moment's notice, a demonic attack showed up in the car. The enemy didn't want me to be FREE. I didn't realize that my freedom was so important to him until the attack showed up for me. It was one thing for God to send reminders of His love but something different when the enemy displays his response to the truth that you got away! I thank God for friends who can pray! I thank God for friends who know the tactics of the enemy and know just where to hit him where it hurts and destroys! I know that had they not been in the car with me and had I been with someone else making that same decision, I probably wouldn't have made it out; in fact, I know that I wouldn't have made it.

Looking back now, it's funny to consider where they were taking me, Pinehurst, a place known for pine trees. Not only are they known for their beauty, but also for their ability to produce and sustain in adverse weather. Like a pine tree, over time and in life I had to learn how to survive through all kinds of places, self-imposed or not, that was never the question.

I had to learn how to make it through the stares.

I had to learn how to make it through the assumptions.

I had to learn how to make it through the disappointment I caused.

I had to learn how to make it, period.

Once we overcame and arrived, the first plan on the books was to shower and get some fresh clothes on. Not only did this day become a fresh start for me, but to my surprise a whole makeover and a day to watch who I was go completely down the drain. I got my nails AND my hair done, something that was more than a hot commodity to me. Unlike the process of getting me in the car, I didn't fight but instead embraced it. I had no other choice. As it was back home, I was confronted with reminders all around – people that God used at a moment's notice just to let me know that He still had me in the palm of His hand. One day while walking home, I remember a man stopped me and told me that God had instructed him to follow me. As I continued to walk, sure enough he continued to follow until I passed out. I don't remember any visions during that time or even dreams, but I do remember the words that uttered out of my mouth – The Lord's Prayer.

[9] In this manner, therefore, pray:

Our Father in heaven,
Hallowed be Your name.

[10]Your kingdom come. Your will

bo dono On oarth as it is in

heaven.

[11]Give us this day our daily bread.

[12] And forgive us our debts, As

we forgive our debtors.

[13] And do not lead us into temptation,

But deliver us from the evil one.

[d]For Yours is the kingdom and the power and the glory

forever. Amen.

Matthew 6:9-13

In times past when I needed help, people simply watched, but I thank God that on this day the man that said he needed to follow me stayed right there with me. "You fainted and I prayed for you," he said, grateful to know that I had come back, for lack of better words.

You're going to be the one to lead them out!

They're going to follow you.

Follow me? Everything in me wanted to stop this man and ask him if he knew how much I had done, but there was no time and even more, no reason to do so at all. My full deliverance did not come in the comfort of a conference or convenient moment, but instead in church. Hear me well, on January 11, 2003, the detox experience that I was afraid of happened for me IN CHURCH. God took the very thing that was afraid of and made it bow in His presence. It was in this very moment that I saw just how weak my addiction was compared to my God! His presence was breathtaking, and I knew that this moment and this time would change my whole life for the best.

This day of deliverance began my sobriety journey. It was here that I began to realize that God not only chose me but wasn't afraid of the mess I was in or had gotten myself into. He wasn't moved by the statistics and what those reports said. God didn't care about how many times I had denied Him before, because in that moment, I received Him, and it was surely by His strength and power.

It was here that I realized that I had finally gone too far and turning back was not an option.

Chapter 9

A Blueprint for the Addict

Yes, my initial deliverance and detox took place in church, but please know, recovery doesn't stop there. One of the hardest truths that I had to accept was that my addiction didn't happen overnight, but instead happened over TIME. I didn't take my first hit and sell all I had that night – I didn't get desperate until my addiction progressed. This habit if you will, is not just something that happens, it is ALIVE, LIVING, BREATHING and MOVING!

Addiction is BIG, ugly and comes with its friends, obsession, and loss of control. Addiction doesn't care about what you look like or even how much melanin you have in your skin – all it cares about is consuming you until there is nothing left! The obsession steps up to drive the addict to whatever lengths are necessary to accomplish their goal while loss of control comes in to remind the addict that no matter how the human body feels, they do not have control as much as they believe that they do. I didn't have control over my original supplier passing away no more than I had control over how people in the neighborhood talked about me and elected me as their choice of entertainment.

Salvation detoxed me.

May I be transparent with you for a moment? Addiction doesn't have "a face." In other words, you can live in the ghetto or prance around in red bottom shoes and still get caught up in addiction. Material possessions and money do not equate to being eliminated or immune from becoming an addict – it just doesn't work that way.

[1]Half of people 12 years old and older have used illicit drugs at least once.

Drug overdose deaths in the United States since 2000 are nearing one million.

The federal budget for drug control in 2020 was $35 billion.

None of the above says that they were black or white only. Nothing shared in the information above says, "well their father did it first, so they were bound to become

---

[1] NCDAS – National Center for Drug Abuse Statistics-
https://drugabusestatistics.org

an addict, too." While this is possible, as some of us may have witnessed (the church calls this a "generational curse") we also realize that addiction will come for whoever is willing. You see for me, getting high was literal. There was something about having that moment in time when everything around me stopped, if only for a moment, just to hear the world on mute. That didn't take having a relative who did the same thing, but merely an opportunity that I said yes to. While you may be reading this and thinking, "I don't have an addiction," I believe that it is just important to understand that these types of decisions don't have to be limited to a drug. No really, anything that stops or causes you to stumble can be known as an addiction.

[7] "You ran well. Who hindered you from obeying the truth? [8] This persuasion does not come from Him who calls you."

Galatians 5:7

What is that thing in YOUR life that has the capacity to slow or stall YOU? Is it gambling, drinking, shopping, smoking, or social media? What is that thing that, when removed from you, throws you into a frenzy? Simply put, what did salvation have to interrupt in your life to get your attention? Whatever that thing was, prior to that moment, not only became an idol but quite possibly your addiction as well.

Remember, you are as sick as your secrets.

Clean versus recovered is the same, right? Sadly, I have to report that it's not. Being clean can last for a moment, take for instance, your clothing. There is nothing like the smell of fresh clothes after they have been washed and tumbled. When you catch it at just the right moment, you may even feel the warmth next to you as you slide it on. By the end of the day or even by the next morning, what was nice and warm just hours ago must now be exchanged for another garment. Why? Because it's dirty. In other words, being clean is a temporal thing! It can last a moment but the chances of lasting a lifetime are very slim. Do you remember that saying, "they clean up well?" Whether you answer be yes or no I want you to bear this in mind – something can look casket sharp on the outside but dead as a doorknob on the inside. Clean is not a FREE ticket to recovery.

Now, when you begin to claim recovery, that holds an entirely different place. It is here that you are ready to admit that you had wholeness in the palm of your hand, but something happened – life or trauma happened! When it seemed as if you had gone too far and could never escape, you found a way to cover "again," or in layman's terms, get back everything that was taken from you in a moment of weakness. This place, this recovery can best be properly demonstrated through this story.

Then he showed me Joshua the high priest standing before the Angel of the LORD**, and Satan[a] standing at his right hand to oppose him. ² And the L**ORD **said to Satan, "The L**ORD **rebuke you, Satan! The L**ORD **who has chosen Jerusalem rebuke you! Is this not a brand plucked from the fire?"³ Now Joshua was clothed with filthy garments, and was standing before the Angel.⁴ Then He answered and**

spoke to those who stood before Him, saying, "Take away the filthy garments from him." And to him He said, "See, I have removed your iniquity from you, and I will clothe you with rich robes."[5] And I said, "Let them put a clean turban on his head." So, they put a clean turban on his head, and they put the clothes on him.

And the Angel of the LORD stood by.

Zechariah 3:1-5

One of the hardest battles I had to fight, was the realization that God had recovered me. In a perfect world, I would have received Jesus as my Savior and all my addictive behaviors would have passed away, but instead, I was found in the constant battle of wondering,

Why did God save ME? Why won't He just let me be?

What did I deserve being chosen?

It wasn't that I was not appreciative of what He had done for me, but there was just something about being chosen when everything else around you says that He should have picked someone else. There were moments when I felt accomplished and powerful and moments when I woke up and was greeted by every doubt and fear that had tried to overtake my mind. Naturally, the greatness that He had called me to and sent others such as Rita to remind me of, was impossible at least in my head. Every part of me fought that elevation before I realized that my best recourse would be to simply, surrender. Who else would be the best fit to ensure my "impossibility" outside of the One who called for it?

23 "Then He said to them all, "If anyone desires to come after Me, let him deny himself, and take up his cross ⒝daily, and follow Me."

Luke 9:23

I can't count how many times I heard that scripture but provided every "reasonable excuse" for why I just couldn't do it. For me, to pick it up once, I could do, but daily, was a stretch. Every day, I would have to wake up and speak over myself. There were some days I stepped into it ready, but other days when it seemed as if every word I was saying was being consumed by the wind, never making it to its destination. I am thankful that I moved outside of the city to gain my deliverance, because I can only imagine how they would have reacted had they seen me getting my life together.

The move for me also caused me to see ME! Michael Jackson had a song called, "Man in the Mirror," where he shared about how he had to look at him first. Honestly, I didn't even want to look at me; I just wanted everything to be fixed once and for all. I didn't want to meet eye to eye with me, only to see the darkness that still radiated from my soul. I didn't want to look at me just to see the Natalie that the neighborhood had come to know and "love." I didn't want to run into my reflection only to realize that though it seemed ready to take on the world, my character defects had just as much power to take me down. It is in this place that we must be routed back God, the one who charged us with massive ability in the beginning. There I was, having to shift from clean to restored, but I could not access it without giving up something and in this case, it was my personal unbelief. In this case, I had to decide that my personal defects and flaws were not too big for God. The same person that puffed up all the reasons why they had to stay in that defeated place forever, ended up being the same one who would have to present their everything to the Father, that is, if she wanted to be totally recovered. It is not enough to simply pick up your cross, but you also must DIE daily.

You must die to your excuses.

You must die to your reasons "why."

You must die to everything you have given power to that tried to take you down and take you out!

When we refuse to do that, we can easily run into a version of our lives that feels like we have fallen victim to the quicksand that has tried to suspend and ultimately overtake us.

"I beseech[a] you therefore, brethren, by the mercies of God, that you present your bodies a living sacrifice, holy, acceptable to God, which is your [b]reasonable service."

Romans 12:1

The very version of you that you may feel is used up, is the very version that God wants! Believe it or not, He can work with You, but you have to trust Him.

What shall we say then? Shall we continue in sin that grace may abound?

Romans 6:1

This is also the place where I had to forsake my pride and release the hope that grace would be there to back me up once again. I learned through this place that my excuses were no good; they were as good as spoiled milk in the dead of summer, and I knew that if I still chose to consume it, God was not obligated to keep me from getting sick. I could no longer use what others said or even my own imperfections as my scapegoat for neglecting the greatness within me. If I wanted God to really use me and really recover me, I would have to present myself to Him so that He could get it out of me!

Chapter 10

A Note to the Family

I will never forget the moment my mother found out about my addiction; her reaction was something that will be embedded in my mind forever. Disbelief took its then, rightful place across her face as confusion began to ask the questions that only a mother could utter.

What made you do that?

Where did I go wrong?

As an addict, to simply agree with her self-interrogation could have been easy, but truth be told I knew that the news she had come into the knowledge of was truly my fault and despite how much she loved me, I knew that I could not allow her to carry this weight. However, I also remember the day when she had enough, and told me that I had to get away from her altogether. At first, I felt abandoned and, in my mind, even thought that I would pull the only child card, but none of that worked. My mother had had enough....

Of watching me struggle.

Of hearing the whispers.

Of seeing me suffer.

She had simply had enough.

In all honesty, I couldn't blame her not one bit, because I was grown and had made a "grown person's decision." The day that she told me to leave, in my mind I wanted to wait and see if the enabler would show up. What is the enabler? By definition, it means, "someone who helps negate the consequences brought on by someone else's behavior." In other words, an enabler is one who finds themselves creating reasons why another person inflicting harm, especially to themselves, is okay when clearly it is not. This relationship can cause one to support an addict's habit and in extreme cases, even go out and purchase the "vice" FOR them. They have also been known for even providing places for the addict to go so that they can enjoy their habit in peace and as crazy as it may sound, in many cases the enabler does not even perceive their movements as wrong or harmful. In our world, the enabler is the one who says,

"I know you don't need it, but if giving you this money to get it will make you feel better, then fine."

In these relationships, the addict is very crafty; they know who they can bring along for this ride. The enabler doesn't want the addict to live like "this," but has made peace with the fact that if this is how they can keep them around, they hesitantly agree to feed into the addiction. Trust me, I tried it. Every card and excuse I could pull to get an enabler on my team, I did it; sometimes it worked and sometimes it didn't. It is my prayer that even as you are reading this, you are looking for the characteristics that have been adopted or initiated in your life, for they are real and can catch you unaware.

Dear Enabler, please do not allow yourself to fall into this trap. Oftentimes, it is hard to find the balance between walking away and enabling itself, but there is a balance and a boundary. Many feel that if they get down on the addict too much, they may lose them forever, but can I say, you must be willing to take that chance. The BEST thing my mother could have ever done on THAT memorable day, was tell me NO MORE! She had done all she could to keep me around but there came a day when she could no longer enable my habit no matter how much she loved me. I knew the process was rough (this was part of my fear in making the transition), but I knew that going back was not an option. The words you just read became not only my truth but my charge, as I embraced what was in that moment and what would be, the unknown, for something I knew was always guaranteed to me, my high.

After years of addiction, I found myself in that cold room full of other people, who shared their names and why they were in the same space with me. Everyone had their separate stories about who they were and what happened to get them in that chair. The only thing that pushed my "share" was knowing that I had nothing to go back to. If I wanted to be free for real, I would need to use every resource available to me, even this. My place in that room, as was understood by my family as well, could not be forced; it had to be desired! In other words, if you want your BEST life, then you will have to WANT what is needed to maintain it! I knew my mother and others loved me, because they tried to save me, but for me this was the best thing I could for myself, to recover simply and powerfully.

It was in this recover process that reality struck – I had done a LOT to maintain this habit. The more sessions I attended, it seemed as if the longer my list of who I needed to make it right with grew. Prior to that day, I would have created and supported all kinds of excuses, etc., but when you realize that is no longer an option, the real work must begin. If only I could just change everyone else, but that was not possible.

I couldn't change what people said or did.

My enablers had to make peace with potentially multiple people because of how they "supported" my habit and movements. This necessary process showed me that I had control of me but had no right to demand controlling others. The saying held true, when these priceless moments hit, it was then that we ALL realized what we were capable of and as a result things about us began to change, even drastically.

Now "back then," talking to a counselor was known as "embarrassing," and sometimes even deemed the person as "crazy." Today though, more people are speaking with and recommending more counselors than ever, especially considering events our nation has endured. Can I encourage you? If and when the need arises, don't be afraid to ASK FOR HELP! Don't be afraid to seek out someone you can talk to and glean from throughout this recovery process. In the process of addiction, it is important to ensure that the individual has a safe place where they can release where they are and what's going on. While some may attend an (NA) meeting, we must also be real enough to admit that the individual may want to do a "home test" version of recovery! Needless to say, HELP is a good thing.

[2]The 12 Steps of Recovery (Narcotics Anonymous)

1. We admitted that we were powerless over our addiction, that our lives had become unmanageable.

2. We came to believe that a Power greater than ourselves could restore us to sanity.

3. We made a decision to turn our will and our lives over to the care of God *as we understood Him.*

4. We made a searching and fearless moral inventory of ourselves.

5. We admitted to God, to ourselves, and to another human being the exact nature of our wrongs.

6. We were entirely ready to have God remove all these defects of character.

---

[2]
https://nasfv.com/bbs/ARCHIVES/Steps_Traditions_Concepts/steps_traditions_concepts.html

7. We humbly asked Him to remove our shortcomings.

8. We made a list of all persons we had harmed and became willing to make amends to them all.

9. We made direct amends to such people wherever possible, except when to do so would injure them or others.

10. We continued to take personal inventory and when we were wrong promptly admitted it.

11. We sought through prayer and meditation to improve our conscious contact with God *as we understood Him*, praying only for knowledge of His will for us and the power to carry that out.

12. Having had a spiritual awakening as a result of these steps, we tried to carry this message to addicts, and to practice these principles in all our affairs.

You can do this. If no one else believes in you, I do.

Chapter 11

Full Circle

There is nothing like elevation, but I won't lie, it is not always the easiest thing to do. This new place is filled with excitement but comes with its own symptoms of what or who you will have to give up for this new place, too.

"Listen! This is my last day out here with you! Don't be out here stealing and robbing these men to get what you want. Today is my last day. Get yourself together because I won't be coming back no more."
Yes, that's exactly what I told them.

When I told my best friend to come back in an hour, she, her husband and maybe even you thought that I asked for more time so that I could have one more rendezvous with my addiction, but truthfully, it was so that I could say goodbye. My addiction brought criticism, but it also brought me a circle of friends, too. No, we weren't doing things "right," but we were doing it together, and for me that carried its own level of fulfillment. Were we perfect?

Obviously not! Did we always get along? Who does? Were we in it for the long haul or at least until the wheels fell off? Surely.

All those days I spent walking past the church in my old neighborhood, I would have LOVED to see just one run out from among them just to let me know that I mattered. Instead, they looked, turned, whispered, while I walked still carrying the thing that hindered me. Had it not been for Rita, I probably would have forever been mad at the church and bitter with God because of how they treated me.

I'm sure someone watching had been abused, too.

Someone among the crowd had gone through depression, too. I wouldn't have even been surprised if at least one looking at me with distain, was at one time a drug addict, too. In that moment, none of that mattered, because none of them would come and get me.

The sad part is that the possibility of housing a Narcotics Anonymous program was once presented, but the churches spoke against the program so much that the addicts left the church and went back to their addictions. Despite the heart of those who wanted to help, the disagreements of the others spoke louder and sent the potentially recovered right back into the streets where they were welcomed, at least in their common community of people. While some would say, "Well they made it this far, why not fight," can you imagine trying to convince an addict of that? For them, it was easier to just give up and go back to their habit than to struggle through the stares and whispers of those who quite possibly, couldn't even relate.

[28] **And we know that all things work together for good to those who love God, to those who are the called according to His purpose.**

Romans 8:28

What the enemy meant for evil, God used it for good! Being rejected by those I wanted to reach out to me didn't feel good, but it birthed something in me that could not be rejected or denied - God commissioned me to call it, "The Reid House." There is nothing like the theory of recovery, but even more, seeing recovery right before your very eyes! When I was high out of my mind, I never imagined God using me like this – I never thought that He would, honestly. The day I started preaching in the same spot I got high in, I knew that everyone thought I had gone mad, but that day, God used that moment as preparation. This vision, I know is well beyond me, but completely possible through the strength and power of my God who has sent me.

R.eaching E.ach I.dividual D.aily

Over twenty million people struggle with addiction but forego the pursuit to get the help they need to recover. Out of those who reach out for help and recover, [3]85% of those individuals relapse within one year while two-thirds return to their addiction within weeks. I have no doubt in my mind that God spared me. All my life, I have been living in the hands of God.

Salvation interrupted my high! It didn't care about what I had done or how dirty I was – it saw purpose in me that I had haphazardly buried. Addiction for me was a hinderance but Salvation saw it as an opportunity....

To save me.

---

[3] https://www.ashleytreatment.org

To redeem me.

To repair me.

To resurrect me.

To RE-present me…. faultless.

Now to Him who is able to keep [m]you from stumbling,

And to present you faultless

Before the presence of His glory with exceeding joy,

To [n]God our Savior,

[o]Who alone is wise,

Be glory and majesty,

Dominion and [p]power, Both

now and forever.

Amen.

Jude 1:24

Resources

[4]How to Stop the Cycle of Enabling:

- Don't lie for anyone. Don't be the parent or wife who gets on the phone and says her husband or son is sick when he's hungover or using.
- Don't make excuses for others when they don't

  fulfill their obligations.

- Don't clean up after a substance abuser. They should see the damage they've done and the chaos they've caused.
- Be accountable for your bills only. If you're not responsible for it, don't pay it. Especially when dealing with consequences that addicts create. Don't bail them out of jail unless they want drug treatment help.

---

[4] "The Enabling Cycle: When Helping isn't Helping"
https://novarecoverycenter.com

- Stand up for yourself. You don't have to be mean, but you do have to put your foot down. Setting and creating healthily boundaries allows you to gain your own life back.
- Don't rescue. A person must suffer the consequences of their actions. Which means don't pay for lawyers or post bail. Many enablers turn from helping to saving and recusing quickly. Soon all of their thoughts and actions surround only the user, and they're missing out on their own life.
- Stop trying to fix everybody. You're not a magician and you're not God. Work on yourself. Get the support of friends, family members and counselors. Join Al-Anon or some other 12-step program. Do whatever it takes to stop yourself from hurting somebody else with your notion of helping.

Substance Abuse and Mental Health Services Administration

Website: https://www.samhsa.gov

Foundation for a Drug-Free World

Website: https://www.drugfreeworld.org

National Drug and Alcohol Treatment Hotline

Phone: 1-800-662-HELP (4357)

Connect with the Author

Natalie Reid

 Apostle Natalie Reid is a wife, mother, servant, survivor, and a Bonafede God's Girl! Born on March 31, 1961, at only three pounds, her parents knew immediately that she was a fighter and destined for greatness. Raised in East Greensboro, North Carolina, Reid attended Catholic School until she begged her parents to attend public school. Needless to say, they obliged!

After years of addiction, Reid gave her life to the Lord in 2003 and was immediately on fire for Him. She found that her most favorite act of service was cleaning the church, as she prepared the house of worship for her leaders and those who would come to obtain the freedom, hope and peace they sought after. She served for ten years under the leadership of Bishop Clyde Sellers. From becoming a youth minister, to Youth Dance Overseer and conference coordinator, she gave every area all she had.

Time progressed, and with this came elevation, from serving in the area hospitality and eventually being ordained Associate Pastor in 2021 and affirmed Apostle in 2022.

More than anything, Author Natalie Reid is a vessel – one who simply wants people to know and receive the truth of who God has been for her and who He desires to be for them. She indeed is a walking MIRACLE and proof that God's Word holds true.

28 And we know [with great confidence] that God [who is deeply concerned about us] causes all things to work together [as a plan] for good for those who love God, to those who are called according to His plan *and* purpose.

Romans 8:28 (AMP)

Made in United States
North Haven, CT
29 August 2024

56688568R00055